The Journey of Love

A COLLECTION OF PASSION FROM A POET'S HEART

OSAGIE OMOROWA

ISBN-10:098907871
ISBN-13:978-0-9890787-1-9

DEDICATION

To the Great Creator, maker of heaven and earth, who bestowed upon mankind a treasure so fare and exhibited triumph beyond what man or angel will ever know...LOVE

CONTENTS

ACKNOWLEDGMENTS

Great praise to The Most High for my lovely dear mother, Josephine and sister, Ruth who encouraged, waited and prayed for me to share with the world what God has given me through spoken word/poetry. You both are priceless, I love you.

I could not forget my dear sister in Christ whom I hold near to my heart, La'Tia. You have been listening and gleaning from the gift God gave to me when no one knew of my name. Your support, both spiritual and natural, is immense! I love you "guuurl!" Thank you!

I dare not leave out another factor that prompted "The Journey of Love." A dear friend of mine, a pupil to the craft of poetry herself, encouraged me to write this particular book long ago. Yes this is overdue. Thank you, Rhonda.

For all who hope, yearn, muse, embrace, and seek love...

INTRODUCTION

Due to what unseen hands have wrought, I would deem myself to be a man of passion, one who seeks to provoke thought and beckon heaven to instill transformation in the hearts of men. Based upon that understanding of oneself I'm honored and pleased to share some mementos from my heart in relation to love, romance, and relationships with you.

Human beings seek love, even the most hardened soul. Some are afraid to open themselves to its prevailing power because they know it can produce change. Sadly, so many have encountered pseudo love and it produced anguish, hatred, and confusion so they locked themselves away from anyone's reach; yet they long for closure, comfort, and care. May we all encounter these blessings. It is my hope that as you read from these pages you will glean from the "ranting" of a passionate heart with purview to promote a paradigm shift.

Welcome to The Journey of Love...

L♦ve

Love is no mere walk through a street called ease. It is a dance, a complexity of movements that takes years to learn and your dance partner at times is the turmoil of life. It is a journey.

~ Osagie

ABSENCE

In the midst of your absence...
I can still hear your laughter in the room
Your voice in the corridors of my mind
Releasing words of life to this seed of mankind
I can still feel your touch caressing my head,
Kissing my cheek and sensing your heat
I see you enveloped in relaxation as I massage your feet.

In the midst of your absence...
I'm comforted by the thought of you
Though you're miles away your lovely face abides in my view
The surge of passion conjuring up in my spirit, soul, and body
Musing upon a woman who dwells in humbleness
And is not haughty.

In the midst of your absence...
You please me
Do please believe me
Thoughts of you so dreamy
One day on one knee
Asking of you to marry me
Till then
In the Spirit cleave to me
Dwell in pure love with me
Walk—with or without me and
Walk this righteous path in jubilee
For in Christ you have already obtained superlative victory

In the midst of your absence...
I can still hear your laughter in the room.

BABE

Babe I'm speechless–
I'm at loss for words
In all truthfulness my love,
I'm honored to be yours.

In my arms is where I desire you to be
Rest your head on my chest
As I caress your back softly
For you to gaze into my eyes
Is what I desire of you even now
To kiss your lovely skin,
As I massage your neck as passion flows through earthly tents

To press my temple against yours
To sense your heart, mine entwined with yours
To taste your passion. To see your tears
To hold you close and whisper life
To slightly move. To draw you near. To feel your groove
To kiss. To love. To laugh. To grasp your hand in mine
To tell you that you are blessed
To tell you, you are my one and only one of God's best–
I'm speechless...

THE BOND

Two born of divine, lovingly entwined
Passion and strength arise—tender touch, closed eyes
Emotion and drive—movement solidifies paradise.

Heart skips
Smooth chocolate hands upon hips
Wrapped in warmth, warding off shivers
Our blood flows vehemently like vivacious rivers
I love you and I will love you forever more
To love you is no chore.

My love for you is rooted in our Great Creator, Christ our Savior
Two born of divine, lovingly entwined
Passion and strength arise—tender touch
Closed eyes.

CONNECTION

Distance conjoined with time yet
Connected beyond temporal,
Far from mundane hands that seek to only mold damnation.
A connection like an estuary,
This is where souls meet and delve
Into the vastness of an intimate sea.

Learning to keep each other afloat,
While delving in the depths of passion,
Yet there is no touch, no words, no piercing eyes
Only two souls meshed like woven yarn.
Two becoming one before time spun a web
To capture their hearts.

They are the quilt telling the story of celestial connection
Inhale and exhale, two elements that bring one factual truth:
Life! He held her before she knew his touch
He was the subtle dew meeting her every morning
He watered her and waited till she bloomed into the realization
That distance and time were but figments of her imagination.

Romance in its purest form is intangible.

~ Osagie

MY LOVE...

MY LOVE...

SO SWEET

MY LOVE...

SO KIND

MY LOVE...

SO PURE

TO YOU

MY LOVE...

WE ARE

DIVINELY

ENTWINED.

CUDDLE—CONVERSING

One blanket, two cups, three jumbo marshmallows; four minutes of cuddle , five minutes of conversing, six minutes of cuddle; seven minutes of conversing, eight minutes of cuddle, nine minutes of cuddle conversing; ten minutes of uhmmm cuddle and uhh I hope that's not too much? Cuz cuddle and conversation go together like hot cocoa and marshmallows ‹chuckles›.

What I'm trying to say is, let me melt into your African American essence with sweet intellect as I penetrate your heart with broken English dialect.

I'm convinced I connect—to places in your spirit where no other has dialed. Smile!
And if they have they got ignored, a dropped line, or a busy tone and left you alone.

I'm tripping, skipping like a kid, yet eyes wide open asking questions I can't overlook—thought I was just a guest signing my name in your book; but it seems my pen was my soul and your book was your heart.

I'm a mess, no disrespect—I'll be sure to stay behind the line, but I won't lie, it drives me crazy how I tingle your spine and I ain't even touched you yet. I honor you. Crossing the line is definitely not about sex, cuz that's been defined. We love our God above our libido drive. High five ‹chuckles›!

All I'm saying is, I won't play your soul like a solo cuz your sound of music is already blissful.

Blessed full is our friendship, can't afford to shipwreck it. You're worth too much to me. Brown gazing into brown. Comfort when I see frowns. Laughter makes like medicine so I clown—I love it when you laugh ‹smile›.

I find it funny whenever you attempt to don a mask, no—I'm not calling you fake, you follow me? I'm just saying like the cliché, that I'm knowing ya like the back of my hand as you walk with me. I'm spitting simplicity, yet composition of words are wrapped so well that I wish I could make them tangible and wrap us in this moment. Delight can be quite overwhelming. I'm buoyant.

EVERYDAY

To be a blessing to you is what I was designed to be
If I was to wait until Valentine's Day
That would be—an utter shame
It would reflect that I was bound
And not walking in the fullness of the unfailing love
The Creator specifically fashioned you to receive
That which emanates from this blood drenched clay
Will forever draw you in baby, everyday.

On every tic
On every toc
When it comes to my love for you
Your man is on overstock
Receiving from the heaven's dock
Every second
Every minute
Every hour will be a witness
To the pure precious love in action
Taking care of business
I don't need your sex
I don't need your money
I don't need to manipulate you to call you my honey!
I refuse to abuse
I refuse to misuse
I refuse to wait until Valentine's Day
To show you, to tell you— I LOVE YOU
I LOVE YOU!

You deserve my affection everyday
You deserve my attention in everyway
You deserve spiritual direction to the place
Where our lovely Creator predestined you to be
And I am that man to cover you, to lead you in fullness of glee.

Everyday I will love thee
Everyday I will kiss thee
Everyday I will seek to be
The man Christ Jesus designed me to be
For you
Everyday.

THE FIRST...

The first rose
The first desire
The first gaze
The first compliment
The first whisper
The first blush
The first touch
The first kiss
The first embrace
The first caress
The first giggle
The first...
The first misunderstanding
The first sadness
The first frustration
The first forgiveness
The first glow
The first prayer
The first...
The first year
The first anniversary
The first of eternity
My love, my beautiful, my precious, my true
My First Love
Sent unto me, you
My love I renew
I give myself to you
The first...

What happens when love extends its hands to nourish and encounters vicious teeth?

~Osagie

SHE COULDN'T SEE RIGHT

So she put on her self—prescribed frames of jealousy
Then turned her dial to 66.6 E—N—V—Y
Fixed her a cup of deception
with a dash of logic—sip, sip, sip, sipping away

Her visage cringed as the tunes delightfully growled at her ears
Her olfactory system whiffed up an aroma,
steaming from the crevices of her heart telling her
That she was mistaken—and she knew,
she knew it was a case of mistaken identity,
but flesh—Flesh beckoned her—sip sip, gulp, sip sip, gulp,

She sat by Brokenness unable to hear its cry
because the tunes played too loud
Yet Pain cried louder and Trust, Trust stepped out on a ledge,
while with veracious intensity Hope begged,
"Don't jump please don't jump everything is okay."

She. She sat on the edge of decision—She sat and she sipped—
and then she leaped and boy did she leap—not as far as she
would've if the production took place on a larger stage,
but leap she did, into the arms of temporary artificial ecstasy.

Sensual lips transmit syllables stylized
with a mélange of memories—Flesh chuckled in speech,
"I got her, but only if the lighting was different."
She gripped the handle of anger
as she plunged her blade of vengeance in the most vital organ,
An organ called love.

The blade delved deep into foreign skin
while those frames hugged her head tight, wrapping itself
Around her ears like wild vines of rage; unable to hear
Hope screaming at the top of her lungs—
"You killed an innocent man, you killed an innocent man!"
She repeatedly stabbed—Her lacerations go unattended.
Thus she must afflict another,
She couldn't see right.

TRUST

It was hard—I know many brothers will not talk about it
Nor admit it, but it was hard
There she lay dying—slowly drifting away
Like rose peddles in the current of dark streaming brooks
It was hard.

I finally understood what the brothers were talking about—
It's hard to find a good woman
The scene is so fresh.
Trust laid there wheezing for breath— clinging to her chest
Without doubt, I knew the perpetrator of this atrocious act
And I, I loved her
I was going to make her my wife
How I wish I could take time as a hostage
And make time take me back
How could she do this to my beautiful Trust?

They should've been the best of friends
Yet, I remember from the inception Trust was suspicious
Giving off vibes that I should
Have nothing to do with that woman
So I sat Trust down and explained
That I've been praying and I'm in love with that woman
And my beautiful Trust nodded her head
And gave me a hug and we proceeded...

I mean I—I didn't know this would happen

It seemed as if they were getting along just fine

I mean—it was Trust

Who convinced me to buy that woman pearls

And the only thing that woman could do

Was take wires of flesh

And attempt to strangle to death my beloved Trust

And now— Here she lays and

 I won't let her go! I won't let her go!

You see she's on hope's life support and I won't pull the plug

It's hard, God knows it's hard, but I—

I got to keep her alive, I know she'll pull through

I just believe, I just believe it— I won't let her go

So please have Trust in your prayers.

As for that monster who committed this crime

 I read a verse that stated, "Vengeance is Mine."

DISAPPOINTED

The fullness of the anatomy of my being bleeds—
The heart of my inner heart cries out to see her free
As she opens wide the gates to her soul as though she was just
Aloof from the proof that she is allowing wickedness to walk in
As if she was death proof she actually holds the rope
While dude's tying the noose.

She's holding the cup while dude's pouring her up poison juice
And though that man wants to kill her and slaughter her seed
She's in denial, thus she still follows like a slave on hands and knees
She doesn't see how precious the Ancient of Days created her to be
Do you see how precious God created you to be?

Her emotions are tragically twisted up like tortuously tangled
Up vines on Amazonian trees waging war against her soul never
To call for a truce she has become her very own noose
That's why she's disappointed.

Humbly, I desire for God to use brothers like me to show them
The pure love of a man who is being molded in the palm of God's
Hand—and I would take her by the hand and speak life in
Abundance by His Spirit that her soul would realize that
Through Christ's grace the pressures of this life,
Yeah—she can endure it!

Eradicate that façade of, "I'm an independent woman"
Some of you are just hiding behind your well paying jobs
Pseudo security and confidence.
Eradicate the façade
Be the woman that is willing to release all the pain within
To the Great physician that dwells within the man that desires to
Be more than an average friend.

The man that refuses to manipulate her to sin
The man that refuses to abuse her like her wicked kin
The man that is patient and yet will speak his mind
For she must understand this man was sent from divine
I'm not politically correct so I speak objective truth—please stop
Running to the woman that wants to be known as Bruce!
She can never take the place of a real man that's walking in Christ's Truth!

You were created to complete man
So while you're lying with another man's rib,
You're missing the whole plan
That's why you're disappointed.

Woman you are the zenith of creation
 The outright Manifestation of Jehovah's declaration of celebration
 That a new Season had come and that man with woman with Him
 Would commune as one.

Though our parents brought a curse upon this holy relationship
There is one that came to correct and restore it
He cursed the curse and has brought new life, new birth
HE healed women who had shattered lives, some demonized, others despised,
He never turned a deaf ear to their cries
Never!

Unintimidated by the haters of his time—He was never ashamed to show to all
that He cherished and loved them—that he respected and honored them
For He came to seek and save them.

I am here to say woman, He came to seek and save you
This ain't no wicked dude that only shows interest to see you
Nude and after he gets what he wants the relationships ensued
No ma'am—He is your one and only hope to go beyond just
Trying to cope to save you from the hell bound slope

Only He can purify your most inner parts and command shame
To depart—so it's not a me nor any mere man you need, It is just
Christ, He is the only Savior.

This is beyond religion this is beyond church
If he can't do it no one else can
There is no other god, there is no woman no man,
It is only the Jesus of the holy script
That can get you out of the bondage that you're in.
CALL ME AN EXCLUSIVIST, I said it,
It is only Jesus the physically resurrected God—man
That can get you out of the bondage that you're in— He is your only hope...
I don't know if you'll have this opportunity again and again and again,
But please let Christ in—and you will not be disappointed.

ALMOND EYES

He's been calling her since she was young
He knew her before she knew she had them almond eyes
Before she donned short skirts to woo men's eyes
Before she warped her tongue into a weapon...He knew her.

And He's been reaching out to her for the longest
He's no extension cord, He is the source
Yet she remains on course trying to find a man
As if that's what's going to make everything ok,

As if that's the piece that's missing
As if he "beating it up" just right will beat her depression away
Her lust away, her low self—esteem away, the fear of rejection away
But it's never gone away that way
So in this circumvented position she stays.

She tweets high praises of herself
But behind closed doors
Her status is "suicide"—if not that, "shame"
Maybe a mixture—maybe her cryptic status is,
"Anger, deep rooted anger"—maybe.
She still be trying to self medicate
Through other means and not just in trying to find a mate
She makes a couple of forward strides yet she is spiritually chained
In other words she remains down and the same
Though outward eyes see her as "on top of the game."

In other words she remains defeated and the same—her heart knows
The broad road is not the way, yet she walks it
She forgot her name, fooled by the fame
Not realizing she's counted amongst the maimed.

Yet, He loves her! He loves her!
Oh how He loves her! Longs to hold her
Her almond eyes that have allured many of men, don't move Him
He knew her before she knew she had them almond eyes.

As a single black man, yes, I just had to put "black" in there ‹smile›, I despise this fallacious belief that many ethnic groups hold to. That black men are wayward bastards who lack self control based upon what some in society have done and western media's portrayal of black men. We can engage in civilized polemics later, ‹smile› all I'm saying is, I refuse for to give one inch of ground to this delusive belief dulcified in order to digress the masses from TRUTH!

~ Osagie

I AM THAT MAN

If I may have audience with the ladies...
You see I serve the one and only living GOD
So you best believe that it's my job
To be a godly man and cover you up
Instead of trying to creep up in your cut
I'm not a squirrel trying to catch a nut
I refuse to play games with precious vessels
Just to put one in the hole like "putt putt."

This is not a mask I'm not an imposter fabricating
Just to have the ladies hold up a, "Vote for O" sign
And get high ratings
Now talk is cheap, but you best believe Christ got his sheep
Men who walk the walk and talk His life
For they hear His voice and follow close by His side
He's placed greatness within us thus in Him we abide.

I am an attractive black man that refuses to comply
With some of your stereotypical mindset
I know this colloquial is out of style but, "Yall got me bent!"
I stand as a voice, as a witness so you can't say you never heard or ever seen
I am not claiming to be the man of your dreams
Not seeking to recruit, "shorty" on my team
So I'll say right now that after I'm done please don't approach me
I'm just here to kill the vibe that says attractive black men only chase hide
Only trying to catch a skeet skeet inside,
That there is none in whom you can confide cuz point blank they all blind!
I'm just here to say, like them old church mothers, "DEVIL, YOU A LIE!"

I represent attractive black men who carry they cross
Who learn to submit to Christ no matter the cost

19

For He is our first love and forever this will last
He's been wooing our soul since eternities past.
You catch that? Let me just spit it plain—
See our spirits will never die
Thus, our eternal—everlasting love for him will always remain.

We are not supermen, and if we were you better believe we'd have a weakness.
There's always some sort of "kryptonite," and sometimes that temptation,
I mean kryptonite comes crashing like tsunami waves full of might,
Pressuring us to give into an overwhelming delusion
A delusion that seems to numb our every sense of accountability to put aside
Our commitment to Christ, our families, and society,
 But praise be to the Ancient Of Days who infused us with his Holy Spirit
To deliver us from our ways.

He reminds us that we are equipped to pass that very test
He reminds us that we have nobody else to blame
And as men we are to take responsibility and put flesh in the flames.

So right then and there when ol' girl looking good
And flesh says, "Swang that wood!"
Right then and there when anger and rage wants to consume
And leave holes in the walls of the room
Right then and there when all hell or whatever is about to break out
The true Superman—the Son of man—the 100% God and 100% man—the Godman
Releases His persevering strength and quickens us up within—
So when the fog is famished and darkness recoils we are still standing alive
And well in the lion's den—because for Him there is no kryptonite, WORD!

We serve the one and only living God
So you best believe that it's our job
To cover you up instead of trying to creep up in your cut
It is our godliness that makes us attractive black men
I am an attractive black man.

RARITY

"It's rare to see," she said. "It's beautiful."

Sends indescribable feelings through the corridors of my soul so I———I don't really know how to describe what I sense.

"It's beautiful."

Its beyond sensual. Spiritual catapults the depths of my being into a celestial comprehension of this matter. Yet to articulate, I shatter. I become undone. I'm—I'm the equivalent of a delicate flower, utilized to lift a ton, it can't be done. I'm at a loss of words—

Ok, maybe this will help. I gaze upon frames encasing its story, its message of hope, its beckoning for more to come rest in its haven, like "come all who are heavy and burden laden." These frames within the frame communicate that we are blessed and I see... I see its truth with such clarity that despite the rarity that it is not a fairy tale, and when spoken of it's not kin to tall tales, nor does it only exist on canvases caressed by cosmetics, No!

It is real, it is here, it is beautiful!

It is soft, it is strong, it is beautiful!

It is here, it is now, it is beautiful!

It is vibrant, it is commitment, it is Black

It is love— Black love

It is beautiful Black love!

I PERCEIVE HER BEAUTY

I perceive her beauty, yes perceive—for it is yet to be seen

It is buried in a celestial womb crying out for her to let go of her wounds

She is beautiful, she is bright, she is black, a precious black woman

With goals and she flows with dreams like milk and honey

Maybe that's why men and women can't see beyond her temporal body and age

Maybe that's why they can't hear her soul

With all the applause they can't hear her soul

Panting, she is thirsty—her imagination says ignore, but it's a thirst that must be quenched

Her spirit needs holy numinous rain, may her being be drenched...and flourish

If she would take time in quietness and face her dark mirror

With the only One that can heal her inner heart for He knows the real her

She will then know freedom

She will then know love

She will then know Him—thus, she will know herself

To touch the sky is what resounds to her core

Yet there is no amount of success that will fill her void

And God wants her to use her gifts and talents

Yet above this—

His heart bleeds for her to know Him beyond religion to a life that's spiritually valid

To go beyond acknowledging to living in that knowledge

To the point she'll lay down her own dreams and flee from ungodly things

Because love in the heart and mind of God is more than a mere word.

ENOUGH IS ENOUGH

Enough is enough, and enough have slept with a dreaded disease.
Dreams filled with fleas yet unable to flee
Due to the shackles around her neck, wrists, and ankles
Forced down to her knees, eyes fixated on the shadow of the beast,
Another pawn in the palm of his hand.

A colored man, imposing a wretched identity upon
Her like old master's perverse hand
Categorize thighs, depends upon how sweet the cherry is in the pie.
The book is black and black is the skin
And it is nothing more than a slave ship
Gruesome acts unfold untold animalistic behavior demands of you
To be driven by the desire to explode
Lust driven to succumb to the delight to cum
You exchange Eve's daughters in orgies to scum after scum
AIDS dribble down her thumb
She's been so misused her emotions are numb.

She's led with the wickedry of trickery
Cursed attractive personalities and she—she in turn leads her seed
Throwing them away to the dreaded disease
So every day she awakens to the tune of, "I hate me, I hate me, I hate me."
Another day just to be a slave, just trying to start a spark
But nothing more than anguish burns in her cave and she and her seed
Are the sacrifices that another black man has laid on an alter
For the god of shame.

I ask why? Why does she relish a reprobate?
Why is she convinced this is her due fate? Why?
Many voices speak, yet she remains silent
But I'm not here to force her to engage in dialogue
So, I'm not moved by her outward silence
Because I—I can hear you wailing from the deep crevices within
You incarcerated the child within, formed another personality
That displays itself to be your protector your friend,
But I—I push aside your facade to tell you I refuse!
I refuse to misuse, to see you woman
As a mere piece of meat to meet my meat.

I am not a black beast sent from the perimeters of hell to feast
Because I—I desire to know you.
I desire to see your face not your face—to listen to your heart's cry
Seeking to escape from your lips and not seek your lips to taste.

And I—I can boldly state this because
 I've been captured by Christ's grace
He's re—altered my taste and to seek strange flesh
Would be a damnable disgrace so in the midst of my refusal I will wait
Wait upon the great architect to show you His design,
To open your eyes to quicken your inner mind, that you may know that
You are more than what you know
That you may know that you are sent from Divine.

I visualize you beyond your current state of being swept away
In the current of hate. "Hate" take away the "h" is what you ate and "ate"
Add a "l"—late. Yes, they say—you say it's too late for you to be rescued
From being initiated in the death rate.
I visualize you beyond the torrent of torment of your current state—
So all I can do is ask—ask of you to allow this black man's hand
To be the branch you grab
You see, the Vine from which I extend has the strength
To ensure your deliverance to stand on dry land. It is not I it is the Vine

You can opt to misunderstand me, but this is not deception.
I'm not spitting these lines to be first in line
To have you at the end of the night.
I'm just spitting raw! You're hearing the heart of a poet
Inebriated with compassion not Moet!
And I pray, yes I pray that your lovely, dovely eyes would realize you are
More than breast and thighs—because enough is enough.

See your worth. See that you were made to be cherished, appreciated, and respected—raise the bar.

~ Osagie

PRICELESS

Beauty evolved, quilted under intimately entwined touches.

Natural inclinations captured essence neutralizing all weariness,

Yoking every ardor, yearning every scent—Inhaling...

Waiting anticipating notable alacrity. Motions of transition occur

Romantic clinging yearning comfort, lips engage...

SHE NEEDS TO HEAR THAT SHE IS BEAUTIFUL

She needs to hear that she is beautiful with no strings attached. Many years ago, my sister told me of those who danced with a fiend called low self—esteem. Though men suffer from this sickness it was insight to women to which she progressed.

Again, many years ago my sister told me of those who danced with a fiend called low self—esteem. I heard this demon sneaks into dreams and tells them their desires will never be. "You are not good enough, pretty enough, your money is not enough—just accept mediocrity. Well even that's too much. How about taking this dagger of lies and lay all confidence in a casket of eternal hush?"

And so my sister proceeds and says to me, "Osagie, life is in the DNA of your voice. Wells spring from your belly. The oasis in your core stem from He who is living water, so give these who thirst drink. NO, you are not the source, many will mistake you to be but KNOW, you are but a vessel filled with the Potter's purifying presence—SO POUR.

Because there are many women who need to know they are loved, they are accepted, they have worth, and they don't have to believe in the deception that says they are lower than dirt. They need to know that there are men, God's men, who lend a hand without the other hand underneath their skirt. They hurt, from red light districts to white—collar turf. They wear masks to accomplish their task, "I gotta play tough so I can last."

"So don't get disgruntled Osagie, you're not here to make them change, just be the God—fearing man who's an agent of change. Keep it simple tell her she is beautiful! Tell her she's beautiful! Tell her she's beautiful!"

So, here I stand with no strings attached. You are not a mistake! Though rejection has bellowed in your soul so loud that your heart birthed a child called callous and though you drink from a chalice that belongs to bitterness, you're still a soul in which He invest.

So let my lips craft a note to slip under your self—made cell door you're so much more. You are beautiful!

And to my sister who knows no sorrow of clinging to her past, but holds fast to the lies sowed by both seen and unseen foes, just know that grace is available to let that burden of comparison go. That oppression of oppressing your true creative ability must no longer be allowed to breath. You are beautiful!

To all women no matter your circumstance,
 I need for you to know you're beautiful with no strings attached. You are beautiful! You Are Beautiful! You Are Beautiful!

IF MY SISTER ONLY KNEW

Sisters: black, white, yellow, brown, red beautiful sisters
I want you to know me, me being the voice of many
Many being men, I want you to know me
The me God created me to be
And the process in which I'm in
To be all He desires of me
First to Him, and in Him is you –His crown of creation
And hopefully you'll dispose of old wives fables
Denounce damnable declarations, assumptions, presumptions and
Other vices of mental corruption.

If my sister only knew, that we too are emotional beings
So don't be duped by the austere stoic faces you're seeing
I weep within and outwardly
Not all are afraid to show emotional growth, transparency
And as we groan don't classify us as weak with no back bone
Because you'll shut the door to what you've been praying for
My structure is strong but my stain glass can still be shattered.

If my sister only knew, that she can't change me
No manipulation, degradation, nor simulation
Will shift my inner propensities
It's a perplexity and the only key to produce a paradigm shift
Is the Holy Spirit's Correctional ability
I'm not saying He can't use you, all I'm saying is
In you of yourself, you can't change me.

If my sister only knew, we need room to make mistakes;
As one man said, "We are Christ—like but not Christ"
This is not a, "get away with it card"
We are to be held accountable for our actions
No room for habitual contradictions,
So do please respectfully confront me
But remember it's not what you say it's how you say it.

If my sister only knew, that relationship wise
I should not have to suffer for the wrong
Other men committed against you
Release them from the jail cell of unforgiveness

Because this baggage impairs our lines of communication
Halting our progression and I need you
Do you hear me? We need you!
And this applies to my sister with same sex attraction,
Despite the deception.

She can never be he and he can never be she
Because we were designed to fit
And fulfill, like rotation to wheel, we move forward
Strengthened by His word, defang the lies you've heard
Extract the poison incurred, be cured, via spoken word
I need you, I'm not saying you're the Christ, but I need you
To be my cleft in the rock so you can rock my soul to sleep
I need you to be my place of safety, imagine with me
A Sampson without the Delilah.

If my sister only knew, I want to trust you
I long to open up the door to my in-depth intricate place of
intimacy—My heart.

If my sister only knew, I am not intimidated by your success
So flourish as Deborah in the shade of your palm tree
I will not oppress but bless your destiny
I will cover you.

If my sister only knew, that honor and respect
Are the two components that create the oxygen to my soul
These produce the best in me, not smart-aleck, disrespectful remarks
That marks against my manhood
I just want to be understood.

If my sister only knew, I want to learn to understand her.
A man once said, "Real men are created but true men are revealed."
So here I am, no longer concealed
Placing pieces of the puzzle in proper position
So the picture is revealed.

If my sister only knew,
We are forever humbly grateful to have you as precious jewels

If My Sister Only Knew.

She was formed, fashioned, and framed to be found by me.

~ Osagie

I WANT TO BE

See, you have to understand that in the midst of all your problems
I want to be your escape
And it's not that I'm fooling myself, attempting to replace
He who created time and space.

Who penned the perfect princess and placed her before my face
Naw, I just desire to be resource from the Source
Made to be a covering, I earned an "A" in the course
Now it's time to apply what's been learned in the real world
Swam through the seven seas to see which oyster had my pearl.

Was one Hades of a fight, but was graced to persevere,
So now I'm standing here asking you
The eighth wonder of the world, to be mine—I want to
Cradle your heart and live within the memoirs
Of your yesterdays, todays, to everlasting eternities
Keeping the continuity of unashamed love advancing
progressively.

 I got security systems in the seat of my emotions
 See, I've recorded your voice, scanned your iris, and fingerprints
 And I know the name and smell or your favorite body lotion
‹chuckles›.

All I'm saying is all other women would be dismissed,
Utterly put to shame, turned away, rejected and
Seen as an attempt to intrude if entry to my heart was sought
For there is no other woman such as you that has been wrought.

And, I know what I'm about to tell you may sound corny,
But uhhh—
I see us like shoe strings–We keep crossing each other's path
And now that we made it to the top lets tie the knot
I'm dedicated to see us last, till death do us part
I want to be.

I SEE IT

I make you wanna catch yourself—catch your breath
Call your best friend and say, "Girl, you better catch me!"
And what's so crazy is the foundation of this bliss
Is not based upon carnality.
I find it attractive when you attempt to
Hide your attraction towards a brother
Our interaction is like no other,
Even when I seek to draw up an intellectual speech, I sputter
My words blush, and that's why at times I just—Gaze upon you
My tongue is telling me to be silent and just take in
Your presence
Your essence
Second by second
I find it attractive when you attempt to
Hide your attraction towards a brother
I can see it, I do–Clark Kent, yet not ordinary dude—
But the world is blind, they know not our kind
They ask, "You get some yet?"
And our final answer is, "NO!"
And it's not that our libido is low,
But spiritual maturity identifies the deeper connection inside
An intimate, intricate, interpersonal relationship
Woven by He who is omnipotent, thus concerning us
He holds authorship
I know I'm jumping ahead of myself, but I can see where this is going
Set sail in the winds of predestination, no rush
But, "Will you marry me?" is our destination
I know I'm ahead of myself, but—I see it
I make you wanna catch yourself—catch your breath
Call your best friend and say, "Giiirl, you better catch me!"

Take in a deep breath, now open your eyes, because this is not a fairy tale. You are not asleep. A vicious trick is not being played. This is real. This is God. This is what love was meant to be—Breathe!

~ Osagie

MAYBE THAT'S WHY

It is said she came from my side
And though I know I'm whole maybe that's why
I feel there's a piece of me missing
And maybe this inner yearning is a type of reopening for her to be
Strategically engrafted within my triune—for fear hinders me no more
And maybe that's why my inner radar is searching for you
The rib that connects, and though I know I'm whole maybe that's why
I say, "No" to those that come my way
I mean, these women would be considered the "trophies" of their time
But they and I don't connect in the Spirit
Because it is said, that's where we first met
Before our natural eyes became mirrors
And our hands entwined displayed the unifying of unique minds
Before our lips of clay birthed forth life
I have always loved you
And you—you have always loved me
You woman, the sweet fragrance of eternities whispers of love
You woman, the tangible glory set before me
You woman, whose essence is sweet, nothing insipid or weak
And maybe that's why I'm preparing myself spirit, soul, and body
And why the Great Physician is working within me—open heart surgery
Why He is anatomizing and emancipating my mind
To ensure that His ways are truly mine
Because you the gift are beyond, "top of the line"
And He won't stand to see you hurt this time
And maybe that's why I'm willing to wait
Why I don't chase various women to date
Maybe that's why I exercise self—control
By not having sex out of marriage
Nor is masturbation riding in my carriage
Yes, it's all for Christ's glory
And He has allowed me to know you fit in this story
I see you, yet I long to see you
I know you, yet I long to know you
I touch you, yet I long to touch you
I love you, yet I long to love you
And though I know I'm whole
I sense there's a piece of me missing
Because it is said that you came from my side
Maybe that's why.

Christ & His Bride

He loves her, so He laid down His all to have her, and to have her, He will, for He fulfilled the zenith of will and willed His will away...She is His.

- Osagie

ONCE UPON A TIME

Once upon a time
I birthed from my womb of creativity
A poem entitled,
"Sweet Loving," to the Lover of my soul, the supreme Deity.

The setting was in the month of February
The people went from store to store in a scurry
It was Valentine's Day
While men were thinking of new pickup lines
The ladies dreamed of a prince charming, oh so divine
I mused and delved in the truth within
That Jesus is my forever "Valentine"
For He dwells within.

Once upon a time
I never thought that I would embrace a woman to call mine
But is it not wonderful that the Lover of my soul could see
That man should not be alone.

That the season would come when you
My Love would be with me
That you My Love would walk with me
That you My Love would pray for me
That you My Love would marry me
For I am yours and you are mine
And we are divinely entwined.

I will one day be a steward of His daughter... I will give account of my faithfulness, according to His standards, of how I handled His precious little girl.

~ Osagie

A PRAYER

God teach me how to love your precious beautiful little girl.

God teach me how to lead her down Your path.

God enlighten me to know her needs no matter how vast.

God anoint me to make sweet love to her spirit and soul

While I wait for her body

You have blessed and restored for me to hold

Lord Jesus, love her through me...love her through me...

Let Your yearning passion burn down in the depths of my
sanctified soul

Let it release, rushing forth and overflowing drenching her in Your
glow

God teach me how to love your precious beautiful little girl.

Discern his heart and learn his soul—receive his all.

~ Osagie

PREMARITAL MIND

I don't need no amour! I need that one godly woman that I truly adore.
I don't want to be no Adonis, dividing my time, going back and forth cuz
Two, three women want to say, "He's mine!"
Only to suffer at the end losing more time.

Though they say, "The sex would be great," but my body ain't mine!
I've been bought with a price, I'm infused with divine
So a paradigm shift has occurred
Not Adonis, but Adonai is with whom I concur.

Strengthened by Him I've resolved to practice what I preach
Eat full portions from the platter from which I teach
Digest and allow it to become one with my soul,
So my one woman will know she ain't gotta worry about
If whether or not I'm coming home.

Authentic Judaeo Christian monotheism manufactures monogamy
Despite hypocrites and the greater number of women in society
Amongst the various ills of society
Such as our men being imprisoned by principalities
I speak to my sisters to rest upon the greater wisdom of the Almighty!

Why lie in the bed belonging to another woman
Proving that infidelity will be your reaping before and after he says,
"Marry me," that's if he say, "Marry me." You follow me?
And for the women that lie with women,
Despite the various pains produced by some men
There is spiritual healing to regain your ground
Your inner being God can mend.
Eliminate the deception that you're a man.
Heterosexual or homosexual,
Being out of the sexual design of YHWH is sin.

So my one woman alone has been allotted the throne to be my aphrodisiac
In her ability to arouse my spirit, soul, and body she never lacks
She is my one and only destination, and believe you me
This is not infatuation,
We committed—We in covenant
We didn't just spit verbiage that was irrelevant.
So to hell with being a Casanova!

Promiscuity don't fit on me
Like my favorite Superman pajamas when I was a kid, them years is over!
And more over, it's not by use of a four leaf clover
That I'm not bending chicks over
It's cuz I got agape word hidden and rooted in my heart.
So my life expresses reverence and not decadence to Jehovah!

It's a connection that many fail to see
Honoring Him causes her to respect and honor me.
Adore Adonai in turn she adores me.
Cuz she sees her Maker
Is making her man be all the man she only dreamed of and needs him to be!
So there's no case of unrequited love, we submit to one another,
Give unto each other, my one and only woman is my lover.

And some say we so saccharine, that our oneness can't be that real
That it must be filled with aniline.
It irritates them to see two souls, healed and sealed with bloody red,
But they don't see the fight.
Relationship is work and to build, you can't afford to depend
On your own might, nor your own power, but they don't want to hear it—
so Let them certified suckers find another host to claim cuz
They can't touch us!

Unseen foes attempt, but continually fail to crush us—cuz
He's crushed us, and mixed us—As One!
Added living water, reshaped us to resemble the bride and His Son.
So why wait until something like "Val–en–tine"
Since I know, I cherish her value–in–time.
I better till the "till" in "till death do us part"
By living with her in wisdom and holding her essence
And not just her body parts!

She's sweet and her sweetness is not just in her kiss
But in her character, so I trust her. You hear me? I trust her!
So her hands hold my heart
That's the reason why she's my sweet heart.
My one—and—only woman.

I want our bodies to become the dance in the moonlight and know that it is pleasing in God's sight

~ Osagie

HUMBLED

It humbles me

It humbles me to know that my smile serenades your soul

It humbles me that you desire to know me, just for me

It humbles me that God's face shined upon our destiny

It humbles me how He assembled our paths to join hands

It humbles me that I'm not alone,

That the feeling that I'm feeling is mutual

It humbles me that you are enjoying this journey

It humbles me.

I WANT TO...

I– I can't even hide it anymore. I was once afraid
But I'm not afraid any more
It's been a long time, but I desire it the more
I want to fall in love again
Grow in love again.

There's just something about that authentic effervescent feeling
That goes beyond one's feelings
Like, when a disagreement occurs,
No longer "seeing eye to eye",
Yet love remains kindled inside.

I want to fall in love again
Grow in love again
I muse upon the time I held her
Who at that time I thought was once mine
Not desiring to reverse time to be reassigned
Because sadly, she was a lie.

It's I reflecting upon the state of my inner heart
My heart that opened wide to allow a woman inside
And man that felt so good, though I was afraid
Man it felt so good!
Though vulnerability became my middle name
Man it felt so good!

It felt so good,
To love
To express
To set my heart to be and become the best heaven could offer
I want to fall in love again
Grow in love again
For I am not afraid anymore.

This woman is within my heart like wind chimes, love blows, melodies flutter like dandelions soft touch yet protect as a lion – I promise.

- Osagie

FLUTTER

Her heart flutters carried by butterfly wings

She feels butterflies in her inside

When his eyes kisses her frame

"Remain calm" are the two pills she pops

As her imagination sets to do the hop scotch,

"Girl, just play it cool," but she's unable to

His deep eyes see her in all her beauty

Spirit, soul, and body.

LAST LINE

Hey baby girl, I sit here thinking of you
Smelling your scent, Victoria Secret perfume
Wanting you in my arms, I write this poem longing for our time
Away from each other to be gone
Listening to you, enjoying your voice
I thank God for choosing you
He made a wonderfully wise choice.

Baby, I love you
And though these may be some of the last lines you read
Know my love will never end for thee
Know my love will always burn for thee
Know my love for you has made its decree that,

I need only one
I need only you
I need your love
Your passion true.

To know you — spirit, soul, and body
To know you as the woman God created for you to be
To know you, a strong secure woman in the Lord God Almighty.

Baby, I'm sitting here in empathy
Recalling all you have shared with me
The pain you have experienced is no small thing
And I pray for your complete healing
I pray for the restoration of years
That the canker, palmer and every other worm have eaten
For you Christ was bruised and beaten
And victory is yours
Because on the right hand of God, Christ is sitting.

Baby, I'm loving you
Baby, I'm hearing you
Baby, just to be near you
Baby, just to kiss you.

Baby, I love you
And though these may be some of the last lines you read
Know my love will never end for thee
Know my love will always burn for thee
Know my love for you has made its decree.

ONLY ONE

I Need Only One
I Need Only You
I Need Your Love
Your Passion True.

I Need You
I Need Your Touch
I Need Your Blush
I Need Your Laughter
I Need Your Tear
I Need Your Prayer
I Need You Near
I Need You.

I Need Only One
I Need Only You
I Need Your Love
Your Passion True.

You love me? How can you love me when you know not He who is Love?

~ Osagie

L.O.V.E.

"I love you." So he said, yet those words that leaped from his lips carried no weight, no umph, and no depth. It was as shallow as a perishing brook whose H2O had left. She's left with emptiness because she mistook that four-letter word to be a towering wave of acceptance, of commitment, of arrival—"I'm here, finally." Only to receive a fine and more penalties. His words never concurred with his actions, yet she stayed and now dwells in disarray.

"I love you." So she said and as she rode, his eyes rolled to the back of his head. Her lips dripped with honey—oh so sensual. Her hips swayed like pendulums prancing on cloud nine. She worked those four-letters like a master hacker and hacked away at his thought process–played this man like recess. He is in a state of denial that her moves were not congruent with her statement, that it was like chess—checkmate! They mate and he is checked off her list.

"I love you." A phrase that holds a four-letter word that some catch as if it's a disease, then attain penicillin to rescue them from the feeling of unease. "I love you." For some it's an acronym for, I Lie, Oppress, Violate & Empty you, but still give me your sex or your money. Loathsome eros.

"I love you." You love me? But another question is, do you even love yourself and is it evident? Don't answer so swiftly take the fifth and think upon this fiercely. Don't approach this like a quickie. If you learn to love yourself then you're in a better position and capable of loving me as a neighbor, phileo—

The crux of the matter is that this four-letter word is mishandled, misused, abused; thus bearing no fruit, no action to back it up, no sacrifice. NO! Purchasing items and sexual encounters will not suffice! See outwardly you connect, yet within your world you decathect from them. Birthed from fear, that is, you disconnect—you withdraw your spirit, your soul. So all they're really holding is a corpse; an empty shell of flesh attached to strings. So that's why there's still soul ties— no lie— its deep huh? Breathe!

"I love you." His actions are harmonious with His words; they fall not to the ground and die, but produce life. The Prince of Peace peering from the balcony of Heaven, He saw and He came then further expressed His love for mankind. He presented faith, hope, and love as a bouquet. Draped mercy and grace upon our necks like adornments. Beckons us to continually find rest and abide in His tent. "He loves me, He loves me not," will never be part of our set. He loves me not 30, 60, but a 100 percent. "I love you." and His words stirs my soul so I must take this conflagrant passion and command us to examine our roles with this four–letter word called L.O.V.E—Agape.

"I love you." that is—I <u>L</u>isten to, <u>O</u>pen up to, <u>V</u>igorously defend & <u>E</u>mbrace you. I must learn to love me, so I may whole-fully love you. That we may love us. That our lips are in sync with Heaven's bliss. L.O.V.E. That our conscious decisions and actions are a reflection of unadulterated L.O.V.E., For GOD IS LOVE and I— love—you!

The crux of the matter is that this four letter word is mishandled, misused, abused and its bearing no fruit. No action to back it up, no sacrifice.

~ Osagie

I have this strange feeling that some of my brothers are feeling left out...well you are...NO, NO! I'm just joking! Look deeper and you will find your story in one of these pages...

~ Osagie

LOVE & SEX

She looked deep into his eyes and said, "Discover me."
"Rip, dig, claw your way out of your fetal mind
That held you hostage and left you dangling from a noose
constructed of lies
That spiked your retina with black thus you're blind to true
beauty
So lust becomes your guide dog to sniff your way into my thighs."
Her eyes were flaming bold
And she told that little boy in the body of a man, "I'm deeper than
that!
You want to feel my wetness, yet you understand not my worth,
From Whom I've been birthed.
I'm cradled deep in my Father's infinite wonders.
Fearfully and wonderfully made
So I will not squander my heart, my life, and my goods away
from bed to bed.
I refuse the deception that says,
"'Well anal and oral are ok as long as missionary is not the position
in which you lay'"
You lie, birthed from the father of lies
I will not be manipulated by minions to forfeit my mission
I am a woman of vision!"

At another place, at another time, another looked at the other and
he said to her,
"My erectile function was not crafted to lead us into corruption,
No pictures of the perversion of scriptures will hang upon the
walls of my heart
Yes, I know He'll forgive, but He also says from sin I should depart
Not part your legs like the Red Sea and delve in freely with no ring
No "swing –batter – batter– swing",
I'm not even stepping up to plate
NO, I'm not a eunuch for the King.
YES, sex is appealing, but you're more than just,' "that thing, that
thing, that thiii–ii–ii–iing!'"

55

And I've slain a Goliath called "Penthouse"
Because this vessel is God's house! I ensconce myself in His house!
Set aside for Him and in Him I'm enabled to identify her.
So to what she just knew to be a "Yes!"
His magic marker revealed a **BOLD**, *italicized, and* <u>underlined</u>, "<u>*NO*</u>"
She doesn't know that he's beating vigorously with massive blows his foe called flesh
And that salve is on his eyes so he sees her for who she is– a wolf in women's clothing
WHAT BIG TEETH YOU HAVE!

Understand that these peculiar ones, they have nothing to lose
But much to gain! Nourished by bread that's unleavened
As they walk in the land of the leaven
Bearing the name of heaven
Understanding they're in, but not a part of a world
That did depart from the Father's heart
So their God is not the pleasure in their body parts
They captured the Creators revelation that copulation
Is an art best begun and mastered in the Master's hand
So Hebrews 13:4, "a" clause manifests in the Master bed
In their veins flow the conviction and eloquence of the text
Because their hearts, minds, and emotions are set on,
Love and not sex!

LOOKING FOR LOVE

She's looking for love, in all the wrong places
She's just trying to find someone to soothe her soul
She's looking for love in all the wrong places
She's just trying to find someone to quench her souls thirst.

I've seen her many of times, in different cities of various shades.
Nappy to straight hair, blonde to brunette all caught in the net of—
Looking for love…

I've seen her before and there she goes again
Every time she rolls them dice, she never wins
Stresses she's grown and sexy
Occupation: From fast food to law firms, she hasn't learned
That all eyes aren't blind
See her in fetal position as she groans, wipes tears then proceeds on—
Looking for love…

Women are from Venus and men are from Mars
So she travels to and fro on the energy of dark stars
Thus she never finds rest
Her frontal lobe doesn't know how to purge itself
Of imprints left by past trauma
She lives in denial, couple that with the current drama contorting her mind
Due to stress, but she's "grown and sexy"
Meaning life has made her grow fast
And she identifies herself through sexual acts
And that's not just for red light prostitutes
Its also for the white collared ones—
Looking for love…

He leaves, then she lets him back in again. Leave, then back again.
It's like sweeping up the exterior of your residence
Then the wind picks up the trash and leaves and
Dumps it on your front porch again
No matter how beautiful, leaves plucked from the source are dead
The relationship is dead, yet there's something
About the touch of the man you love
Grown and sexy wants to get her groove back like Stella
Go out with the girls to try looking for love…

But she's invested so much in this fool,
So when he waves that ticket for re—admission
She lets him in hoping something new will birth
So sad that during his absence she never took time
To find and embrace her worth
So she keeps pressing replay looking for love though she knows
The entrance to her heart is not under her skirt
Her means to reach bliss becomes her hurt
Again he's snatched away by red lingerie across the way,
This other chick is another one—
Looking for love…

She told me she doesn't search for love anymore because bitterness
Took its needle and the thread of sorrow and sowed her eyelids shut!
So she just gonna, "live" and never put her hopes up
Cuz she never wins the bid whenever she was looking for love
Her life is tick, tick, ticking away so she like,
"Whatever! Who gives a f**k!"
And she doesn't care if you do though you do.
She feels like you must be doping up if you do
Because as far as she's concerned, sincere love is as real as a dodo bird,
Extinct.
"Why take another chance of being hoodwinked
When I can just cuddle up with a drink?"
On the pathway to her heart, she sits as a Grecian sphinx,
Answer her riddles right or wrong you will still suffer death for—
Looking for love…

She tucked herself away as a lost cause
There is only one person I know that can take her callous heart
And revive her again, but as for now depression is her dearest friend
It'll "love" her till the bitter end
I've seen her many of times, in different cities of various shades.
Nappy to straight hair, blonde to brunette all caught in the net of…

Looking for love in all the wrong places
She's just trying to find someone to soothe her soul
She's looking for love in all the wrong places
She's just trying to find someone to quench her souls thirst.

We've heard it said, "Everything that glitters ain't gold"... well, everyone that smiles and says the right thing ain't a potential spouse.

~ Osagie

NOT ALONE

Hear her thoughts
Sometimes it seems like I will forever be alone
Is any brother seeking to be a godly man?
Is any brother out there taking a stand?

It seems like every brother just wants to get buck wild
Catch'em at the bar, swing a couple of rounds,
Then catch'em a pretty lady and lay her on down;\
Hate on other brothers—exchange frowns or buck rounds.
That's what it seems to be, as though
They just roll with an animalistic flow.

Lord, is there anybody, specifically brothers who is not tricking, sticking
they baby mamas older daughter?
Who do not see women as prey and would rather
restore than be a part of the slaughter?
Who breaks the cycle of Section 8, whereby, other brothers may see
that you can make it despite how the system seeks to manipulate?
That it's not a dream when you're determined to get out the game?
Who humbly calls on Christ to release them from the wretched chains in
their mind?

Are there any brothers seeking Your face Lord?
Who refuse to use the drama between him and his baby's mama
As an excuse not to pay child support?
The child doesn't even know daddy lives next door or down the street
because daddy says dealing with baby is obsolete
Who refuses to use his dad's feasting on crack as a reason to batter the
woman he says he loves?

Lord, I hope I'm not sounding selfish, but I desire a godly black man
But it seems as though there are none taking a stand!
It's as if the "good ones" are already taken
I'm not desperate and I refuse to lower the standards You have given me
I know I have You and yes, I have embraced that You are all I need
Yet in this moment of all out honesty
I cannot hide this from Thee
I don't want to forever be—alone.
Lord, is any brother seeking to be, continually, a godly man?

Attention! Attention all women, every man that opens the door is not subtly saying open your legs. Chivalry still exist. Thank you, you may now proceed.

- Osagie

I am not intimidated by your success. So flourish as Deborah in the shade of your palm tree. I will not oppress but bless your destiny—I will cover you.

- Osagie

INSECURITY

She – She is not, but he is
She blooms in the storms and the fragrance of her success
paralyzes his pride.

And he– he is so unsure of what will occur, so he wastes no time
to attempt to degrade her and he hides behind his penis and
presents himself to be the cure because he–
He is insecure.

Look! Look at that woman, upright, short, tall, bronze like,
burgundy like, olive like, xanthous like, chocolate like, peach like.

Look at her, a queen. A queen regenerated in her spirit abiding in
Christos esteem in her, of herself she will not lean.
And he—he parades his falsified image of manliness, while within
the seat of his soul churns bitterness because a seed was sown and
matured because he—
He is insecure.

She is scaling up a celestial ladder in tune with divine. An unseen
hand guides her like an august artist's brush swaying upon the
canvas. She is a beautiful display of predestination.
And he—he fails to grasp the concept of true greatness of true
leadership, that it is not born of flesh nor of the will of man, but
conceived by the epitome of Pure, yet he cannot see because he—
He is insecure.

And I'm not even speaking of "independent status."
There is a 34 –year– old man intimidated by a 12- year- old girl,
Because he sees the drive in her eyes to show the world, she is a
precious pearl.
And he—he dare not lay a finger on her because she dares to be the
seed to prevail against his wickedry
Because she is wise enough to discern he is an enemy,

that seeks to take her purity, to cause her to deviate from the process of inner prosperity
Enroll her within the misery of maturity becoming that 30 year old woman with tormenting thoughts thumping, "He stole from me! He stole from me!"
All due to his insecurity.

Talitha cumi, Talitha cumi
Arise, arise damsel, arise. And wear your tiara, head held high.
Move with the vigor of victory in your stride.
The truth is that your God—given greatness and that man's internal insecurity will always collide, but realize Celestial sovereignty
solidified success through one sacrifice!

Wrapped in rigor mortis due to the choice not to abort us
Love, the stimulus.
Concerning freedom, the Genesis
Resurrection was the Exodus
The fulfillment of rigorous requirements of Leviticus
I dare not be ambiguous, I speak of Jesus!

And because of Him and Him alone, destiny beckons you to press on regardless of your past.
You're like—like home made well preserved jam.
Your beauty remains sweetly unique and like former and latter rains, your grandeur will fill barren lands.

So bloom, bloom in the storms and let the fragrance of your success paralyze his pride because you, you are woman and he—he is a child—

Insecurity.

Do you truly understand that your spouse holds key components concerning your destiny?

~ Osagie

WARMTH

The warmth of the sun has kissed your horizon

Is it real, yet surreal?

Is it concrete, yet abstract?

Is it tangible, yet you wait to touch?

As of now you bask & allow the rays entrance

To massage your being.

You can feel

You can feel my touch

While we read lines from the script of our hearts

Yet not a play, but two energies that prayed

Now embracing the answer

Both being in blessedness

Because that one moment shifted it.

SHE KNOWS

You see it was not good for man to be alone and so
She became the crescendo of creation,
Crowned in perfection by Perfection.
Visual—unbelievable,
Spiritual—invaluable,
Man was responsible—
"You're bone of my bone and flesh of my flesh,"
But somewhere along the way
He let his guard down and opted to disobey and so...

Here we are
At the crossroads of attempting to put things back together
Failure after failure,
Insisting on doing things our way instead of the Living Way
Just like our first parents.

And as it was for them God comes to mend us
Revealing the mediator between God and men, Jesus.
And now that we have Him all I'm saying is we can began again
I cannot promise you the Garden of Eden,
But I can promise you the Promised Land of understanding me.
You see I want your ear to become the stethoscope to my heart,
Its open to you, follow its every beat
I will interpret the rhythm so we can move our feet in sync.
And if there's an inability to hear,
These hands will become students of sign language
To beckon you near.

And if your vision is impaired,
I will be the Braille, which leads you to me.
Just know I'm here, and I care, and I've disposed of ungodly codes
So, I won't implode nor explode, yet there is one thing that
bother's My soul—

What will she do with what she knows?
Because the song is no longer, "If she only knew"

The song is, "What will she do?"
Seeing that God has graced you to attain information
That men are NOT from Mars and women are NOT from Venus,
but from His womb of creation.

And He is the bridge connecting our psychological uniqueness
We don't have to give into indifferences
I mean what good is it if we gather around,
And exchange smiles while all along our soul dons a frown?
What is it?
Are we too afraid to trust that God really wants to heal us?
Too afraid to admit our assumptions are wrong?
Too afraid to let go of our past to press forward through Christ
and be strong, strong enough to be vulnerable with one another
And discover the true beauty of a wholesome godly relationship?

My sisters, hear the words of life from this brother
And refuse to eat the fruit of learning and not applying.
There are too many who are malnourished in truth and are dying.
Eat of Christ's life and you will find your being arising,
Realizing there is more to life than waiting for a man
To take your hand.

For God will bless the works of your hands—
All I'm saying is continue to live a productive life as you're waiting,
Being a hearer and doer of God's Word spoken
Through some of the vessels you've heard
Yes, SOME! Because you dare not receive from all,
You must discern.

For the enemy still snickers concerning Eve
And how he fooled her.
Opt not to fall for the same deception of the deceiver!
You're a believer, so believe you me
That this is beyond you just knowing about me.
Me being men, this is about the woman
Growing beautifully within!

Look into her eyes— soul to soul, sow life into her present, annihilating her past and welcoming harvest in her future—Look into her eyes and speak these words, "I give you my trust, I give you my affection, I give you my time, I give you my heart, I give you my love, only wrap me in your bosom of forever as I cover you providing surety for your soul that I am yours alone." Look into her eyes.

~ Osagie

RELEASE YOURSELF TO ME

Release!
Release yourself to me
Release...
Release your cares to me
Release...
Release your fears to me
Release...
Release your tears to me
Release...
Release your all
To the very last drop of
Your passion
Release...
To the earnest cry of your soul
Release...
Let me cover you baby
Release...
Let my love for you
Overshadow the full essence of your being
Oh, baby...release
Release yourself to me
My love
My precious
My beautiful
Release...
For I am
Your priest
Your protector
Your provider
Your pleasure
Release...
Release yourself to me
Release!

QUOTES

- Let not the sweet lips upon many daggers manipulate and cause you to deviate from the sensitive places of one's heart.

  - Osagie

- Our fallen nature has corrupted our desire within, and the games we play have never fixed it.

  - Osagie

- God is love and His love is the zenith of exquisiteness.

  - Osagie

- I wish... I wish I could speak with the tongue of an angel to let you know how celestial our love is.

  - Osagie

- Woman you are the zenith of creation— the outright manifestation of Jehovah's declaration of celebration that a new season has come and that man with woman with Him would commune as one.

  - Osagie

- She is cradled deep in her Father's infinite wonders. She is fearfully and wonderfully made, so she will not squander her heart, her life, her goods away.

  - Osagie

- What is it? Are we too afraid to trust that God really wants to heal us, or admit our assumptions are wrong, or let go of our past to press forward through Christ and be strong? Strong enough to be vulnerable with one another and discover the true beauty of a wholesome godly relationship?

  - Osagie

- She is scaling up a celestial ladder in tune with divine an unseen hand guides her like an august artist's brush swaying upon the canvas. She is a beautiful display of predestination.

  - Osagie

- I've seen her many of times, in different cities of various shades. Nappy to straight hair, blonde to brunette all caught in the net of looking for love in all the wrong places.

  - Osagie

- I'm not claiming to be the man of your dreams, not seeking to recruit you on my team. I'm just saying there are men who have been redeemed...Everyone ain't acting a fool.

  - Osagie

OSAGIE OMOROWA

For Booking and Contact Information:
Please visit
WWW.OSAGIE.NET

9 780989 078719